THE OFFICIAL ASTON VILLA ANNUAL 2012

Compiled by Rob Bishop and Ruth Pepler

A Grange Publication

© 2011. Published by Grange Communications Ltd., Edinburgh, under licence from Aston Villa Football Club. Printed in the EU.

Special thanks to Gayner Monkton and Lorna McClelland

Photographs © Neville Williams, Getty Images and Action Images

ISBN 978-1-908221-18-6

£7.99

CLUB HONOURS

European Cup
Winners: 1982
Quarter-finalists: 1982-83

European Super Cup
Winners: 1982-83

World Club Championship
Runners-up: 1982

Intertoto Cup
Winners: 2001

Football League
Champions: 1893-94, 1895-96, 1896-97,
1898-99, 1899-1900, 1909-10, 1980-81
Runners-up: 1888-89, 1902-03, 1907-08,
1910-11, 1912-13, 1913-14, 1930-31,
1932-33, 1989-90

Premier League
Runners-up: 1992-93

Division Two
Champions: 1937-38, 1959-60

Division Three
Champions: 1971-72

FA Cup
Winners: 1887, 1895, 1897,
1905, 1913, 1920, 1957
Runners-up: 1892, 1924, 2000

League Cup
Winners: 1961, 1975, 1977,
1994, 1996
Runners-up: 1963, 1971, 2010

FA Youth Cup
Winners: 1972, 1980, 2002
Runners-up: 1978, 2004, 2010

CONTENTS

marc
ALBRIGHTON

SHAY AIMS for 40

Villa had never had a 40-year-old player until Brad Friedel achieved the feat in the final match of last season. Now Shay Given is aiming to follow suit after becoming the club's new goalkeeper during the summer.

The Republic of Ireland international has some way to go, having turned 35 in May. But the five-year contract he agreed when signing from Manchester City will take him past his 40th birthday in May 2016.

"If you do the right stuff in the gym and look after yourself, you can play a lot longer, especially as a goalkeeper," says Shay. "My aim is to play for as long as I can. Brad Friedel did fantastically well and Villa fans will be grateful for the service he gave the club. He had a fantastic time here so hopefully I can do something similar and be a reliable source behind the defence.

"I have not come here to rest up, I have come here to prove I am a top Premier League keeper. I'm grateful to get that length of contract but I believe I can play for many more years - even beyond that."

It's a well-known fact that goalkeepers tend to continue playing far longer than their outfield

> "MY AIM IS TO PLAY FOR AS LONG AS I CAN."

counterparts and numerous keepers have played well into their 40s.

Shay intends to do just the same, and he admits he was excited when he learned Villa wanted him following Friedel's move to Tottenham Hotspur.

"Once I knew there was interest from Aston Villa I was determined to get here. This is a club with a fantastic history and a great fan base."

Shay began his career as a youth player with Scottish giants Celtic before moving to Blackburn Rovers. And although he only played a few games for the Ewood Park, he helped Sunderland to win promotion to the top flight during a loan spell with the Black Cats in 1995-96.

The following year he joined Sunderland's big North East rivals Newcastle United and played more than 400 games for the Magpies before being transferred to Man City in 2009. Hopefully he will play plenty of games for Villa before reaching that magical 40th birthday!

Charles *loves* VILLA PARK

Charles N'Zogbia was described by manager Alex McLeish as "explosive" when he signed for Villa from Wigan during the summer. But the stylish French midfielder is happy to adopt a softly, softly approach.

Charles saves his explosive performances for the pitch. Off it, he is a shy, retiring character who doesn't make a big deal about his abilities.

"I play the way I play," he said. "I just want to improve on my game and if the manager thinks I'm explosive, that's great. I want to do my best for this club. I'm delighted to have joined a club like Villa. It's a big step in my career.

"I had always enjoyed playing at Villa Park before I came here, so I'm looking forward to playing lots more games over the next few years. It's an exciting time for me. I will just try to do my best and hopefully we will be successful."

Villa's manager had been a big admirer of N'Zogbia for quite some time and even tried to sign him when he was manager of Villa's Second City neighbours Birmingham City. That transfer never materialised, although there is clearly a mutual respect between player and manager.

"I'm just happy he has signed me for Villa," said Charles. "He's a strong manager who knows what he is doing. Together with the other players I hope we will be able to take the club forward and achieve something."

The stylish Frenchman is also pleased to have been reunited with another summer signing, goalkeeper Shay Given, the duo having previously been team-mates at Newcastle United.

"It was good to link up with Shay again," he said. "When I heard he had signed for Villa I was really happy. He helped me when I joined Newcastle and he's a very good goalkeeper."

"It's also great that we have such good attacking players in Darren Bent, Emile Heskey and Gabby Agbonlahor. I would love to set up some goals for them but I was Wigan's leading scorer last season so I also want to score a few myself!"

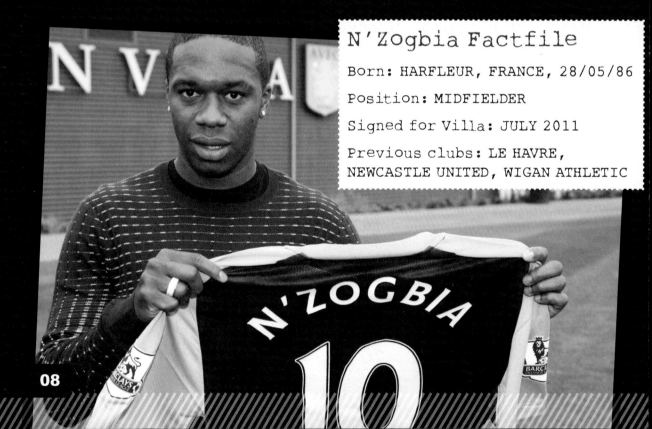

N'Zogbia Factfile

Born: HARFLEUR, FRANCE, 28/05/86

Position: MIDFIELDER

Signed for Villa: JULY 2011

Previous clubs: LE HAVRE, NEWCASTLE UNITED, WIGAN ATHLETIC

a far east ADVENTURE

Villa headed for Hong Kong during the summer – and the trip was a huge success both on and off the pitch.

While the players warmed up for the new season with Barclays Asia Trophy games against Blackburn Rovers and Chelsea, club officials used their Far East adventure to promote the claret and blue cause in that part of the world.

A number of Hong Kong trams were covered in Villa imagery, while all 12 of the Star Cruise line's ships now have club merchandise on board.

The club took over the Nike store in Kowloon – the new kit was so popular that many surrounding streets had to be closed! On the pitch, Villa beat Blackburn 1-0 in the semi-final with a Darren Bent goal before losing 2-0 to Chelsea in the final.

Q&A with... marc ALBRIGHTON

MARC ALBRIGHTON MADE HIS BIG BREAKTHROUGH IN THE VILLA TEAM LAST SEASON – AND COULDN'T STOP WINNING AWARDS. BY JANUARY HE WAS ASSURED OF THE LIONS CLUB'S TERRACE TROPHY, HAVING WON FIVE OF THE FIRST SIX MONTHLY AWARDS, AND HE COLLECTED THREE MORE TROPHIES AT THE CLUB'S ANNUAL AWARDS DINNER. HE TELLS US ABOUT PLAYING FOR THE CLUB HE SUPPORTS...

You grew up as a Villa fan?

Definitely! I had no choice really because my dad Terry is a Villa fanatic. I was born in Sutton Coldfield although we moved to Tamworth when I was a baby. Apart from going to Villa games, I played for junior teams and I joined Villa's Academy when I was eight after being spotted by Clive Lyons, one of the club's scouts. Clive died a couple of years ago but I will always be grateful to him.

Who was your hero when you were a boy?

Dean Saunders. He was Villa's main striker when I was very young and I used to love watching him score. I had a replica shirt with number nine and the name Deano on the back – Saunders wouldn't fit because the shirt was very small! I was even nicknamed Deano, although that stopped after I left school.

Have you always been a winger?

No. When I first played football I used to play up front. I scored a few goals, too, but I didn't grow as quickly as I would have liked. I was playing for Villa's Academy teams by then and it was suggested that I might do better on the wing.

How about your first team debut?

It was in March 2009 against CSKA Moscow at the 50,000-capacity Luzhniki Stadium, where Manchester United had beaten Chelsea on penalties in the previous year's Champions League final. Unfortunately the stadium was half empty when Villa played there and we lost 2-0 – but it is something I will be able to tell my kids about!

How did it feel to win so many honours last season?

It was great; I got the Supporters' Player of the Year award, shared the Players' Player award with Ciaran Clark and had my goal at Fulham voted Goal of the Season – but Barry Bannan's long pass deserved a lot of the credit. I also won the Terrace Trophy, which is voted for by the supporters' clubs. The honours which have given me most satisfaction were winning the league with Villa's Academy and reserve teams when I was younger.

What was your best moment of the 2010-11 campaign?

The one that really stands out was scoring against Manchester United. It was my first goal at Villa Park for the first team and to score it at the Holte End against a team like United was amazing. It made my mum and dad very proud, too. Some of my friends told me later that it brought a tear to mum's eye when I scored.

What advice would you give to youngsters who want to be professional footballers?

Work hard, but you also need to be totally dedicated. Some school friends were talented footballers, but when things got tough, they didn't have the dedication to work their way through it. Any young player is bound to have setbacks at some stage. It's all about how you deal with those setbacks.

What are your ambitions?

I want to be a regular in the Villa team for many years to come – and it would be nice to play for England! I want to test myself at the highest level.

THE VILLA FILES

Name
Shay GIVEN

Personal Information

Born: LIFFORD, IRELAND, 20/04/76

Position: GOALKEEPER

Signed for Villa: JULY 2011

Previous clubs:
BLACKBURN ROVERS, NEWCASTLE UNITED,
MANCHESTER CITY

Name
Andy MARSHALL

Personal Information

Born: BURY ST EDMUNDS, 14/04/75

Position: GOALKEEPER

Signed for Villa: AUGUST 2009

Previous clubs:
NORWICH CITY, IPSWICH TOWN,
MILLWALL, COVENTRY CITY

2010-11 record:
APPEARANCES - 0

Name
Brad GUZAN

Personal Information

Born: CHICAGO, USA, 09/09/84

Position: GOALKEEPER

Signed for Villa: AUGUST 2008

Debut: QPR (h) Carling Cup 24/09/08

Previous clubs: CHIVAS USA

2010~11 record:
APPEARANCES ~ 3 cup

Name
Richard DUNNE

Personal Information

Born: DUBLIN, IRELAND, 21/09/79

Position: CENTRAL DEFENDER

Signed for Villa: AUGUST 2009

Debut: BIRMINGHAM CITY (a) 13/09/09

Previous clubs: EVERTON, MANCHESTER CITY

2010~11 record:
APPEARANCES ~ 32 league, 3 cup

Name
James COLLINS

Personal Information

Born: NEWPORT, 23/08/83

Position: CENTRAL DEFENDER

Signed for Villa: AUGUST 2009

Debut: BIRMINGHAM CITY (a) 13/09/09

Previous clubs: CARDIFF CITY, WEST HAM

2010~11 record:
APPEARANCES ~ 31 (1 sub) league,
                2 (3 sub) cup

GOALS ~ 3 league

Name
Stephen WARNOCK

Personal Information

Born: ORMSKIRK, 12/12/81

Position: FULL-BACK

Signed for Villa: AUGUST 2009

Debut: BIRMINGHAM CITY (a) 13/09/09

Previous clubs:
LIVERPOOL, BLACKBURN ROVERS

2010-11 record:
APPEARANCES - 19 league, 3 cup

Name
Habib BEYE

Personal Information

Born: PARIS, FRANCE, 19/10/77

Position: FULL-BACK

Signed for Villa: AUGUST 2009

Debut: WIGAN ATHLETIC (h) 15/08/09

Previous clubs: PARIS ST GERMAIN,
STRASBOURG, MARSEILLE, NEWCASTLE UNITED

2010-11 record:
APPEARANCES - 3 cup

Name
Luke YOUNG

Personal Information

Born: HARLOW, 19/07/79

Position: FULL-BACK

Signed for Villa: AUGUST 2008

Debut: MANCHESTER CITY (h) 17/08/08

Previous clubs: TOTTENHAM HOTSPUR,
CHARLTON ATHLETIC, MIDDLESBROUGH

2010-11 record:
APPEARANCES - 23 league, 1 cup
GOALS - 1 league

Name

Carlos CUELLAR

Personal Information

Born: MADRID, SPAIN, 23/08/81

Position: CENTRAL DEFENDER

Signed for Villa: AUGUST 2008

Debut: LITEX LOVECH (a) UEFA Cup, 18/09/08

Previous clubs: NUMANCIA, OSASUNA, GLASGOW RANGERS

2010-11 record:
APPEARANCES - 10 (2 sub) league, 5 cup

Name

Nathan BAKER

Personal Information

Born: WORCESTER, 23/4/91

Position: FULL-BACK

Signed professional: SEPTEMBER 2008

Debut: WIGAN ATHLETIC (a) 25/01/11

Previous clubs: NONE

2010-11 record:
APPEARANCES - 4 league, 1 cup

Name

Stiliyan PETROV

Personal Information

Born: MONTANA, BULGARIA, 05/07/79

Position: MIDFIELDER

Signed for Villa: AUGUST 2006

Debut: WEST HAM (a) 10/09/06

Previous clubs: CSKA SOFIA, CELTIC

2010-11 records:
APPEARANCES - 23 (4 sub) league,
                2 (1 sub) cup
GOALS - 1 league, 1 cup

Name
Fabian DELPH

Personal Information

Born: BRADFORD, 21/11/89

Position: MIDFIELDER

Signed for Villa: AUGUST 2009

Debut: WIGAN ATHLETIC (h) 15/08/09

Previous club: LEEDS UNITED

2010-11 record:
APPEARANCES - 4 (3 sub) league,
                1 cup

Name
Marc ALBRIGHTON

Personal Information

Born: TAMWORTH, 18/11/89

Position: MIDFIELDER

Signed professional: NOVEMBER 2007

Debut: CSKA MOSCOW (A) UEFA Cup, 26/02/09

Previous clubs: NONE

2010-11 record:
APPEARANCES - 20 (9 sub) league,
                3 (2 sub) cup
GOALS - 5 league, 1 cup

Name
Jean II MAKOUN

Personal Information

Born: YAOUNDÉ, CAMEROON, 29/05/83

Position: MIDFIELDER

Signed for Villa: JANUARY 2011

Debut: WIGAN ATHLETIC (a) 25/01/11

Previous clubs: LILLE OSC,
                OLYMPIQUE LYONNAIS

2010-11 record:
APPEARANCES - 7 league

Name
Barry BANNAN

Personal Information

Born: GLASGOW, 01/12/89

Position: MIDFIELDER

Signed professional: JULY 2008

Debut: HAMBURG (a) 17/12/08

Previous clubs: NONE

2010-11 record:
APPEARANCES - 7 (5 sub) league, 7 cup
GOALS - 1 cup

Name
Darren BENT

Personal Information

Born: LONDON, 06/02/84

Position: STRIKER

Signed for Villa: JANUARY 2011

Debut: MANCHESTER CITY (h) 22/01/11

Previous clubs: IPSWICH TOWN, CHARLTON ATHLETIC, TOTTENHAM HOTSPUR, SUNDERLAND

2010-11 record:
APPEARANCES - 16 league
GOALS - 9 league

Name
Gabriel AGBONLAHOR

Personal Information

Born: BIRMINGHAM, 13/10/86

Position: STRIKER

Signed professional: FEBRUARY 2005

Debut: EVERTON (a) 18/03/05

Previous clubs: NONE

2010-11 record:
APPEARANCES - 17 (9 sub) league, 6 cup
GOALS - 3 league, 2 cup

Name
Emile HESKEY

Personal Information

Born: LEICESTER, 11/01/78

Position: STRIKER

Signed for Villa: JANUARY 2009

Debut: PORTSMOUTH (a) 27/01/09

Previous clubs: LEICESTER CITY, LIVERPOOL, BIRMINGHAM CITY, WIGAN ATHLETIC

2010~11 record:
APPEARANCES ~ 11 (8 sub) league, 4 (2 sub) cup
GOALS ~ 3 league, 3 cup

Name
Nathan DELFOUNESO

Personal Information

Born: BIRMINGHAM, 02/02/91

Position: STRIKER

Signed professional: FEBRUARY 2008

Debut: HAFNARFJORDUR (a) 14/08/08, UEFA Cup

Previous clubs: NONE

2010~11 record:
APPEARANCES ~ 2 (9 sub) league,
            2 (4 sub) cup
GOALS ~ 1 league, 1 cup

Name
Ciaran CLARK

Personal Information

Born: HARROW, 26/09/89

Position: CENTRAL DEFENDER

Signed professional: JULY 2008

Debut: FULHAM (h) 30/08/09

Previous clubs: NONE

2010~11 record:
APPEARANCES ~ 16 (3 sub) league, 3 cup
GOALS ~ 3 league, 1 cup

Name

Andreas WEIMANN

Personal Information

Born: VIENNA, AUSTRIA, 05/08/91

Position: STRIKER

Signed for Villa: AUGUST 2008

Debut: WEST HAM (h) 14/08/10

Previous clubs: NONE

2010~11 record:
APPEARANCES ~ 0 (1 sub) league,
0 (1 sub) cup

Name

Chris HERD

Personal Information

Born: MELBOURNE, AUSTRALIA, 04/04/89

Position: MIDFIELDER

Signed professional: JULY 2007

Debut: MANCHESTER UNITED (h) 13/11/10

Previous clubs: NONE

2010~11 record:
APPEARANCES ~ 1 (5 sub) league, 1 cup

Name

Jonathan HOGG

Personal Information

Born: MIDDLESBROUGH, 06/12/88

Position: MIDFIELDER

Signed professional: JULY 2007

Debut: RAPID VIENNA (a) 19/08/10

Previous clubs: NONE

2010~11 record:
APPEARANCES ~ 5 league, 2 cup

SEASON REVIEW 2010-11

AUGUST

There's a massive pre-season shock as Martin O'Neill, Villa's manager for the past four years, announces his resignation just five days before the opening Barclays Premier League match.

Kevin MacDonald, the club's popular reserve team coach, takes over in a caretaker capacity and the players respond with an emphatic 3-0 opening day victory over West Ham at Villa Park.

The stadium is buzzing as Stewart Downing and Stiliyan Petrov give the boys in claret and blue a two-goal interval lead before Marc Albrighton brilliantly sets up number three for James Milner, who is playing his final game for the club before joining Manchester City.

The following Thursday, another piece of Albrighton creativity sets up Barry Bannan's first Villa goal in a 1-1

draw away to Rapid Vienna in a Europa League qualifier – but after the euphoria of a successful opening week, Villa come down to earth with a bump.

A 6-0 defeat by Newcastle at St James Park is followed by an exit from Europe, Villa losing 3-2 at home to Rapid in the second leg after twice leading through Gabby Agbonlahor and Emile Heskey.

It means we have gone out of the competition to the same opposition in the same round for the second year running, but any despondency is soon dispelled by an excellent 1-0 home win over a fine Everton side.

Although the visitors enjoy the lion's share of the play, Villa's battling performance is rewarded by a rare goal from full-back Luke Young, who calmly slots the ball home with his left foot.

AT A GLANCE

DATE	OPPONENTS	V	RESULT	SCORERS
Aug 14	West Ham United	H	3-0	Downing, Petrov, Milner
Aug 19	Rapid Vienna (EL)	A	1-1	Bannan
Aug 22	Newcastle United	A	0-6	
Aug 26	Rapid Vienna (EL)	H	2-3	Agbonlahor, Heskey
Aug 29	Everton	H	1-0	L Young

SEPTEMBER

Gerard Houllier is appointed as the club's new manager, although he has to wait a while before taking over because he is still under contract to the French Football Federation as their technical director.

While Villa wait for the former Liverpool boss to take charge, the team slip to a 2-1 defeat at Stoke City, conceding two late goals at the Britannia Stadium after going ahead with a superb diving header from Stewart Downing.

Kevin MacDonald's final match in charge ends in a 1-1 home draw against Bolton Wanderers after Ashley Young opens the scoring with a superb shot.

After watching that game from the stand, the new boss takes charge for a Carling Cup-tie against Blackburn Rovers four days later, marking the occasion with a 3-1 success. Young scores twice, with substitute Emile Heskey also on target.

The following Sunday, Downing opens the scoring against Wolves at Molineux and although the home side equalise, Heskey's perfectly-placed late header secures a 2-1 Villa verdict.

Meanwhile, Young and Petrov are on opposite sides at Wembley as England beat Bulgaria 4-0 in a European Championship qualifying game. Marc Albrighton scores on his England under-21 debut after going on as a substitute against Lithuania.

AT A GLANCE

DATE	OPPONENTS	V	RESULT	SCORERS
Sep 13	Stoke City	A	1-2	Downing
Sep 18	Bolton Wanderers	H	1-1	A Young
Sep 22	Blackburn Rovers (CC)	H	3-1	A Young 2, Heskey
Sep 26	Wolves	A	2-1	Downing, Heskey

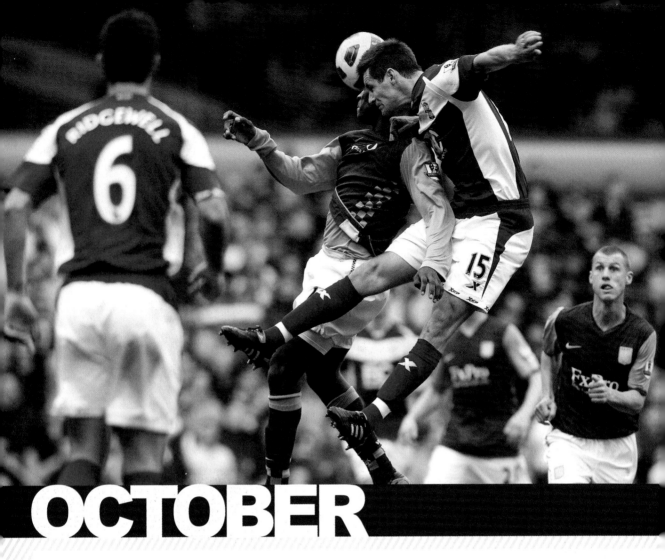

OCTOBER

The phrase "super sub" is often overused, but Villa have two of them in the fourth round Carling Cup-tie against Burnley.

The game is deadlocked at 0-0 until five minutes from the end, when substitute Emile Heskey converts Ashley Young's low centre – only for the visitors to grab a last-gasp equaliser.

That dramatic late equaliser means an additional half-hour, and another Villa substitute, Stewart Downing, powers home a 96th-minute shot to clinch a passage to the fifth round.

In Barclays Premier League games, Villa discover that goals are hard to come by. Marc Albrighton nets his first senior goal for the club, converting Heskey's low centre at the far post, to open the scoring against Tottenham Hotspur at White Hart Lane – but Villa lose 2-1.

There are also goalless draws at home to Chelsea and neighbours Birmingham City, but the team slip to a 1-0 defeat by Sunderland at the Stadium of Light.

Ashley Young, meanwhile, makes his first competitive starting appearance for England in a goalless Euro 2012 qualifier against Montenegro at Wembley.

AT A GLANCE

DATE	OPPONENTS	V	RESULT	SCORERS
Oct 2	Tottenham Hotspur	A	1-2	Albrighton
Oct 16	Chelsea	H	0-0	
Oct 23	Sunderland	A	0-1	
Oct 27	Burnley (CC)	H	2-1	Heskey, Downing
Oct 31	Birmingham City	H	0-0	

NOVEMBER

With several senior players injured, it's time for some of Villa's promising youngsters to display their talents, although the manager also recruits former Arsenal and France midfielder Robert Pires for his experience.

An injury-hit Villa side are involved in three consecutive games which involve late goals. Leading Fulham through Marc Albrighton's clinical finish – a goal created by Barry Bannan's magnificent long pass – they are pegged back by Brede Hangeland's stoppage time equaliser at Craven Cottage.

Then James Collins heads an 89th-minute goal to clinch 3-2 victory over Premier League new boys Blackpool, who had twice fought back to cancel out goals from Stewart Downing and Nathan Delfouneso.

The following Saturday, an Ashley Young penalty and an Albrighton strike put the team two-up at home to Manchester United, only for the visitors to hit back for a 2-2 draw.

Pires makes his debut in a 2-0 defeat by Blackburn at Ewood Park and a week later he makes his first home appearance against his former club. Sadly, it's not an occasion to remember as Villa lose 2-4 to the Gunners, although Ciaran Clark, playing in midfield because of the club's injury problems, has the consolation of scoring his first goals for the club.

Bannan makes his debut for Scotland in a 3-0 friendly victory over the Faroe Islands at Aberdeen, while Ashley Young wins his 11th England cap in a 2-0 Wembley defeat by France.

AT A GLANCE

DATE	OPPONENTS	V	RESULT	SCORERS
Nov 6	Fulham	A	1-1	Albrighton
Nov 10	Blackpool	H	3-2	Downing, Delfouneso, Collins
Nov 13	Manchester United	H	2-2	A Young (pen), Albrighton
Nov 21	Blackburn Rovers	A	0-2	
Nov 27	Arsenal	H	2-4	Clark 2

23

DECEMBER

Villa endure a truly bleak mid-winter, the depression being lifted only by a single victory over neighbours West Bromwich Albion. Even the festive season is far from merry, a Boxing Day home defeat by Tottenham Hotspur being followed by a 4-0 thrashing at Manchester City two days later.

The month could hardly start in worse fashion, Villa's dream of reaching the Carling Cup final for a second consecutive season being wrecked by a 2-1 defeat by Birmingham City at St Andrew's, despite the fact that Gabby Agbonlahor maintains his impressive scoring record against the old enemy from across the city.

That's followed by a 3-0 defeat at Liverpool, although Villa bounce back with a 2-1 home win in the derby against the Baggies, Marc Albrighton's crosses setting up the goals for Stewart Downing and Emile Heskey.

But 2010 ends on a bitterly disappointing note. Following the postponement of the pre-Christmas game at Wigan, the team suffer two festive setbacks.

Marc Albrighton scores against Tottenham – just as he had in the corresponding match at White Hart Lane in October – but it isn't enough to prevent a 2-1 home defeat by Tottenham, and Villa hit rock bottom at Eastlands, where they are completely outplayed.

AT A GLANCE

DATE	OPPONENTS	V	RESULT	SCORERS
Dec 1	Birmingham City (CC)	A	1-2	Agbonlahor
Dec 6	Liverpool	A	0-3	
Dec 11	West Bromwich Albion	H	2-1	Downing, Heskey
Dec 26	Tottenham Hotspur	H	1-2	Albrighton
Dec 28	Manchester City	A	0-4	

JANUARY

It's an exciting, dramatic start to the new year as Villa draw 3-3 against Chelsea at Stamford Bridge.

In a real classic in west London, Gerard Houllier's team trail 1-0, go 2-1 ahead through an Ashley Young penalty and an Emile Heskey header, and then fall behind 3-2 towards the end. It looks as if they are going home with nothing – until Ciaran Clark nods home Marc Albrighton's stoppage-time centre to earn a morale-boosting point.

Unfortunately, Villa follow up with a 1-0 home defeat at the hands of Sunderland, but a late James Collins equaliser earns a 1-1 draw in the Second City derby at St Andrew's before the third week of January is dominated by the club record signing of Darren Bent from Sunderland.

Bent's debut is one to remember, too – he scores the only goal in a 1-0 home win over high-riding Manchester City. A few days later, another new signing, Cameroon midfielder Jean II Makoun, makes his debut in a 2-1 success at Wigan.

In the meantime, Villa hit the FA Cup trail with a 3-1 third round victory at Sheffield United, the scoring being opened by full-back Kyle Walker, who has joined us on loan from Tottenham. There's also a 3-1 win in the fourth round, this time at home to Blackburn Rovers, with Robert Pires scoring his first Villa goal.

AT A GLANCE

DATE	OPPONENTS	V	RESULT	SCORERS
Jan 2	Chelsea	A	3-3	A Young (pen), Heskey, Clark
Jan 5	Sunderland	H	0-1	
Jan 8	Sheffield United (FAC3)	A	3-1	Walker, Albrighton, Petrov
Jan 16	Birmingham City	A	1-1	Collins
Jan 22	Manchester City	H	1-0	Bent
Jan 25	Wigan Athletic	A	2-1	Agbonlahor, A Young (pen)
Jan 29	Blackburn Rovers (FAC4)	H	3-1	Clark, Pires, Delfouneso

FEBRUARY

There's no doubt about the highlight of this month – it's a 4-1 home victory over Blackburn Rovers, featuring a very special goal.

When Ashley Young drills home a penalty to put Villa ahead four minutes after half-time, he scores the club's 500th Premier League home goal. And that goal paves the way for a convincing Villa victory, even if there's a touch of fortune about the second goal as Marc Albrighton's cross-shot deflects in off defender Grant Hanley for an own goal.

Stewart Downing adds number three before the visitors reduce the deficit – and then sets up number four for Young.

That emphatic win makes up for a frustrating time earlier in the month. Darren Bent's second goal for the club fails to prevent a 3-1 midweek defeat by Manchester United at Old Trafford and the following Saturday Villa have to settle for a point in a 2-2 home draw against Fulham.

Fulham defender John Pantsil gives Villa the lead with an own goal in this game – the second consecutive season he has put the ball in his own net at Villa Park – with Kyle Walker charging through the visitors' defence for our other goal.

There's also a draw against Blackpool on Villa's first visit to Bloomfield Road since 1975. This time it's 1-1, Gabby Agbonlahor opening the scoring before the Seasiders equalise just four minutes later.

AT A GLANCE

DATE	OPPONENTS	V	RESULT	SCORERS
Feb 1	Manchester United	A	1-3	Bent
Feb 5	Fulham	H	2-2	Pantsil og, Walker
Feb 12	Blackpool	A	1-1	Agbonlahor
Feb 26	Blackburn Rovers	H	4-1	A Young 2, Downing, Hanley og

MARCH

Perhaps we should call it March madness. Former manager Martin O'Neill managed only a couple of wins during this particular month over the course of his four years in charge – and Gerard Houllier encounters similar problems.

It's a sparse month anyway, with Villa playing only three games. But each one ends in defeat as the team make their exit from the FA Cup and suffer two Barclays Premier League defeats to leave themselves just one point above the relegation zone.

It all starts to go wrong at Eastlands, just four days after Villa's impressive home win over Blackburn. A weakened team crash 3-0 to Manchester City in a fifth round Cup-tie and they find it difficult to regain their momentum over the course of the

subsequent two fixtures.

Darren Bent opens the scoring against Bolton Wanderers at the Reebok, and although the Trotters hit back with an equaliser just before half-time, Villa look set for three points when Marc Albrighton re-establishes the lead and they are then awarded a penalty.

But Ashley Young's spot kick is saved by goalkeeper Jussi Jaaskelainen and Bolton gratefully accept the chance to hit back for a 3-2 win.

In the only other March fixture, Villa slip to a 1-0 home defeat at the hands of neighbours Wolves. It's the first time the Molineux men have won at Villa Park for nearly 31 years.

AT A GLANCE

DATE	OPPONENTS	V	RESULT	SCORERS
Mar 2	Manchester City (FAC5)	A	0-3	
Mar 5	Bolton Wanderers	A	2-3	Bent, Albrighton
Mar 19	Wolves	H	0-1	

APRIL

Darren Bent is in deadly form against Everton at Goodison Park, scoring two smartly-taken second half goals to put Villa in front after they trail to a Leon Osman strike at the interval.

With an away win looking imminent, however, Everton are awarded a controversial late penalty and Leighton Baines converts it for a 2-2 draw.

If a single point is something of a disappointment, though, the result on Merseyside is the first in a sequence of four without defeat for the boys in claret and blue.

They follow up with a 1-0 home success over Newcastle United, James Collins netting the winner with a curling header from Ashley Young's free-kick, and then beat West Ham United 2-1 at Upton Park.

After a slow start, in which Robbie Keane puts the Hammers ahead, Villa hit back to equalise through Bent, with substitute Gabby Agbonlahor heading a stoppage-time winner.

Another Bent goal, this time a precision header from 12 yards, earns a 1-1 home draw against Stoke City but Villa are then beaten 2-1 at The Hawthorns – our first defeat at the hands of West Bromwich Albion for 26 years.

AT A GLANCE

DATE	OPPONENTS	V	RESULT	SCORERS
Apr 2	Everton	A	2-2	Bent 2
Apr 10	Newcastle United	H	1-0	Collins
Apr 16	West Ham	A	2-1	Bent, Agbonlahor
Apr 23	Stoke City	H	1-1	Bent
Apr 30	West Bromwich Albion	A	1-2	Meite og

MAY

All's well that ends well, so the saying goes – and there's no doubt that Villa finish the 2010-11 campaign on a high note.

Going into May, they are still in 13th position and are still not mathematically certain of avoiding relegation. Three games and seven points later, they boast a respectable position in the top half of the table.

The first game of the month is, admittedly, something of a disappointment. Wigan Athletic have not lost in five previous Barclays Premier League visits to Villa Park, and the Latics extend the unbeaten sequence to six by heading home with a 1-1 draw.

The Lancashire club take an early lead through star man Charles N'Zogbia, leaving Villa having to be content with a point after Ashley Young works a short free-kick routine with skipper Stiliyan Petrov to drive home the equaliser.

If the boys in claret and blue never get into their stride in that match, though, it's a different story at the Emirates Stadium eight days later.

Villa really turn on the style against Arsenal to record a memorable 2-1 victory, Darren Bent netting twice in the first 15 minutes to take his total number of Villa goals to nine in 15 games since arriving from Sunderland.

And just when we think it can't get much better, it does! In the final match of the season, Stewart Downing's unstoppable shot clinches a 1-0 home win over Liverpool – and lifts Villa to a finishing position of ninth.

AT A GLANCE

DATE	OPPONENTS	V	RESULT	SCORERS
May 7	Wigan Athletic	H	1-1	A Young
May 15	Arsenal	H	2-1	Bent 2
May 22	Liverpool	H	1-0	Downing

29

IT FIGURES!

BARCLAYS PREMIER LEAGUE 2010-11

	P	W	D	L	F	A	GD	Pts
1 Manchester United	38	23	11	4	78	37	+41	80
2 Chelsea	38	21	8	9	69	33	+36	71
3 Manchester City	38	21	8	9	60	33	+27	71
4 Arsenal	38	19	11	8	72	43	+29	68
5 Tottenham Hotspur	38	16	14	8	55	46	+9	62
6 Liverpool	38	17	7	14	59	44	+15	58
7 Everton	38	13	15	10	51	45	+6	54
8 Fulham	38	11	16	11	49	43	+6	49
9 Aston Villa	38	12	12	14	48	59	-11	48
10 Sunderland	38	12	11	15	45	56	-11	47
11 WB Albion	38	12	11	15	56	71	-15	47
12 Newcastle United	38	11	13	14	56	57	-1	46
13 Stoke City	38	13	7	18	46	48	-2	46
14 Bolton Wanderers	38	12	10	16	52	56	-4	46
15 Blackburn Rovers	38	11	10	17	46	59	-13	43
16 Wigan Athletic	38	9	15	14	40	61	-21	42
17 Wolverhampton W.	38	11	7	20	46	66	-20	40
18 Birmingham City	38	8	15	15	37	58	-21	39
19 Blackpool	38	10	9	19	55	78	-23	39
20 West Ham United	38	7	12	19	43	70	-27	33

FACTS AND FIGURES

- League position - 9th
- FA Cup - Round 5
- Carling Cup - Quarter-finals
- Leading scorers -
  Darren Bent, Ashley Young (9)
- Most league appearances -
  Brad Friedel, Stewart Downing (38)
- Biggest win - 4-1 v Blackburn Rovers (H)
- Heaviest defeat - 6-0 v Newcastle United (A)
- Highest home attendance - 42,788 v Liverpool
- Average home attendance - 37,220

DEBUTS

Andreas Weimann v West Ham (h)

Eric Lichaj v Rapid Vienna (a)

Jonathan Hogg v Rapid Vienna (a)

Stephen Ireland v Newcastle United (a)

Chris Herd v Manchester United (h)

Robert Pires v Blackburn Rovers (a)

Kyle Walker v Sheffield United (a)

Darren Bent v Manchester City (h)

Jean II Makoun v Wigan Athletic (a)

Nathan Baker v Wigan Athletic (a)

Michael Bradley v Blackpool (a)

To be the best footballer you can be, you need to be quick in your mind as well as quick on your feet! Try these and see if you can beat your friends...

SUDOKU

4	2		
		2	4
3	1		
		1	3

The basic rules of Sudoku are easy. Just place the digits from 1 to 4 in each empty cell. Each row, column, and 2 x 2 box must contain only one of each of the 4 digits.

ODD ONE OUT

A ★	B V
C E	D ⬡

Three of these shapes are in the Aston Villa crest, but one isn't... can you figure out which one it is?

MAZE

32

To check if you're right, have a look on page 60.

GOALS, GOALS, GOALS!

VILLA SCORED SOME AMAZING GOALS LAST SEASON, AND FIVE WERE SHORT-LISTED FOR THE GOAL OF THE SEASON AWARD.

That title eventually went to Marc Albrighton's magnificent effort in a 1-1 draw against Fulham at Craven Cottage – with Barry Bannan also making a significant contribution.

The Scottish midfielder's lofted 50-yard ball was arguably the pass of the season, and Albrighton controlled the ball superbly with his right foot on the right-hand corner of the penalty area. In one sweeping movement, he eased past Fulham defender Carlos Salcido to stroke a perfectly-placed left-foot shot beyond goalkeeper Mark Schwarzer and into the far corner of the net.

While that goal was voted number one, the others were also pretty special – including Marc's 76th-minute effort in the 2-2 home draw against Manchester United.

It was a perfect example of a classic counter-attack. Bannan was involved once again, starting the move deep in his own half with a pass to Ashley Young who, in turn, sent Stewart Downing racing down the left.

With United's defence opened up, Downing delivered an inviting centre – and the unmarked Albrighton provided a clinical finish which gave keeper Edwin van der Sar no chance.

The other three contenders were all superb headers – Downing's lunge to convert a Gabby Agbonlahor cross in an early-season game at Stoke City, Emile Heskey's precision finish from Stephen Warnock's centre against Wolves at Molineux and Darren Bent's perfectly-placed 12-yard header from a Kyle Walker cross in the home match against Stoke.

gabriel
AGBONLAHOR

THE DEBUT DOZEN

12 players made debuts for Villa last season but their names have become jumbled up. Can you identify the Debut Dozen by solving these anagrams?

To help you along, the names you are looking for are:

Darren Bent	Kyle Walker	Andreas Weimann
Jean Makoun	Chris Herd	Jonathan Hogg
Barry Bannan	Stephen Ireland	Eric Lichaj
Michael Bradley	Nathan Baker	Robert Pires

1
NANNY BARBAR
★★★★★
★★★★★

2
TEND HER SPANIEL
★★★★★★★★
★★★★★★★

3
SHRED RICH
★★★★
★★★★

4
ENTER BRAND
★★★★★★
★★★★

5
MAN, RISE AND WANE
★★★★★★★★
★★★★★★★

6
BRIE PORTERS
★★★★★★
★★★★★

7
O A MEAN JUNK
★★★★
★★★★

8
JAR CHIC LIE
★★★★
★★★★★

9
HARK - A NET BAN
★★★★★★
★★★★★

10
CHAMBER IDEALLY
★★★★★★★
★★★★★★★

11
WEEKLY LARK
★★★★
★★★★★

12
OH JO! HANG GNAT?
★★★★★★★★
★★★★

Write your answers on a piece of paper. To check if you're right, have a look on page 60.

35

fabian
DELPH

DARREN'S DILEMMA...

Villa striker Darren Bent is keen to learn about some of Villa's top stars of recent years.

Can you help him fill in the blank boxes, based on the clues below? To make things a little easier, we have provided each player's Christian name and the first letter of his surname. (To check if you're right, have a look on page 61)

1. Lee H------, a Birmingham-born midfielder who was sent off on his debut in 1995.

2. David P----, scored a spectacular goal at the 1990 World Cup finals in Italy.

3. Peter C-----, a towering striker.

4. Garry P-----, a 1990s midfielder who joined us from Nottingham Forest.

5. Peter S---------, a goalkeeper who actually scored for Villa.

6. Mark D------, a Welsh full-back who played in the 2000 FA Cup final.

7. Gareth B----, an England star who left us to join Manchester City.

8. Peter W----, scorer of our 1982 European Cup-winner.

9. Nigel S----, goalkeeping hero from the same game.

10. Ian T-----, once a player, now a club ambassador.

37

TIME TO RELAX

Villa's players have to work hard to maintain peak fitness, but what do they enjoy when the training session is over and it's time to relax? We asked a few of the players to reveal a few of their favourite things.

DARREN BENT

SINGER	Robin Thicke
GROUP	Jagged Edge
ACTOR	Will Smith
ACTRESS	Queen Latifah
GAME	Streets of Rage
TV PROGRAMME	True Blood

CIARAN CLARK

SINGER	Drake
GROUP	Swedish House Mafia
ACTOR	Kiefer Sutherland
ACTRESS	Megan Fox
GAME	Call of Duty
TV PROGRAMME	24

CHRIS HERD

SINGER	Bob Marley
GROUP	S Club 7
ACTOR	Will Farrell
ACTRESS	Angelina Jolie
GAME	Mario Kart
TV PROGRAMME	Home & Away

ANDY MARSHALL

SINGER	Michael Buble
GROUP	Coldplay
ACTOR	Liam Neeson
ACTRESS	Megan Fox
GAME	Golf
TV PROGRAMME	Only Fools & Horses

jean II
MAKOUN

SPOT THE DIFFERENCE

There are five things different in these pictures... can you spot where they are?

To check if you're right, have a look on page 61.

WHO AM I ?

See if you can identify these Villa players from the clues about them.

Award yourself three points if you guess correctly on Clue A, two if you get it after Clue B and one after Clue C. Why not test your knowledge against a Villa-supporting friend – but no sneaking a look at the answers in advance!

1. A   I'm originally from London.

   B   I joined Villa from a northern club.

   C   I became Villa's 70th England international early in 2011.

   Guess who?!

2. A   I started my career in my homeland and then played in another country before coming to England.

   B   I have five children – including twins.

   C   I played in the Champions League last season.

   Guess who?!

3. A   I started my career with a club based in a capital city.

   B   A few years ago I helped my former club to an FA Cup semi-final win at Villa Park.

   C   I captained my country for the first time in March 2010.

   Guess who?!

4. A   I've been at Villa since leaving school.

   B   I made my debut in a famous German city.

   C   I made my full international debut in November 2010.

   Guess who?!

5. A   I started my career with the club I supported as a boy.

   B   I missed a lot of last season after suffering a serious knee injury towards the end of the 2009-10 campaign.

   C   I don't like ghosts – and when I joined Villa I left my hotel after a few hours after being told it was haunted!

   Guess who?!

6. A   I scored the winning goal on my Villa debut.

   B   I once helped my club to a treble triumph.

   C   When I scored my first home Villa goal I was wearing a white shirt.

   Guess who?!

barry
BANNAN

THANKS, DAD!

DARREN'S SO GRATEFUL FOR WORDS OF ADVICE

Darren Bent became Villa's record signing when he arrived from Sunderland for a reported £18m last January.

He soon started knocking the goals in, scoring on his debut against Manchester City and hitting nine in 16 games by the end of the season.

But the former Ipswich, Charlton and Tottenham striker appreciates that his success may not have been possible if he hadn't listened to his dad when he was younger.

Mervyn Bent, who had played youth football for Wimbledon and Brentford, knew exactly what to tell his son when it came to advice about his career – steer clear of the booze.
My dad said me : 'Listen, Daz, if you want to give yourself the best opportunity, you've got to be dedicated and make certain sacrifices – and one of those things is not to drink.'

"I've been in the game a long time now but my dad's words are always spinning around my head. That's something I've never forgotten."

Darren's parents parted when he was 10, but they have both given him 100 per cent support throughout his football life. "When they split up I went to live with my mum but it never stopped my relationship with my dad," says Darren.

"He used to sometimes drive me from London to Cambridgeshire and then take me across to Ipswich to training, which was a four-hour round trip.
He wouldn't get in until 4.00am and then he'd have to be up for work at eight. His dedication to me was brilliant, and my mum's was, as well.

"She would have to take on a couple of jobs sometimes to be able to get me to training and I'm very grateful for that.

> **...IF YOU WANT TO GIVE YOURSELF THE BEST OPPORTUNITY, YOU'VE GOT TO BE DEDICATED AND MAKE CERTAIN SACRIFICES...**

"They are still good friends and they travel to every part of the country to watch me. One of the reasons I came to Aston Villa was the geography. It means I'm only an hour and a half from my dad, who lives in London, and an hour away from my mum, who lives in Cambridgeshire.

"It means I can pop and see her during the week. From Sunderland it was a three-hour drive.
You have to take things like that into consideration. My family are close to me – they're an important part of my life. For me to succeed in football, I need them around me."

VILLA'S TRANSFER TRAIL

Darren may have cost a reported £18m but Villa's first record signing cost just £100!

To be fair, that was a lot of money in October 1888, when Archie Goodall joined the club from Preston North End.

Since then, Villa's transfer record has been broken more than 40 times. By 1980, the figure had risen to £500,000 when Peter Withe arrived from Newcastle United – and although it was nearly nine years before that figure was beaten, the fees paid for players have rocketed in recent times.

VILLA'S RECORD DEALS OVER THE PAST THREE DECADES:

COST?	WHO?	FROM?	WHEN?
£500,000	PETER WITHE	Newcastle	May 1980
£650,000	IAN ORMONDROYD	Bradford	Feb 1989
£1.5m	TONY CASCARINO	Millwall	Mar 1990
£1.6m	DALIAN ATKINSON	Ipswich	July 1991
£1.7m	EARL BARRETT	Oldham	Feb 1992
£2.3m	DEAN SAUNDERS	Liverpool	Sept 1992
£2.5m	GARETH SOUTHGATE	C Palace	July 1995
£3.5m	SAVO MILOSEVIC	Partizan	July 1995
£4m	SASA CURCIC	Bolton	Aug 1996
£7m	STAN COLLYMORE	Liverpool	May 1997
£9.5m	JUAN PABLO ANGEL	River Plate	Jan 2001
£9.6m	ASHLEY YOUNG	Watford	Jan 2006
£12m	JAMES MILNER	Newcastle	Aug 2008
£18m	DARREN BENT	Sunderland	Jan 2011

JV LIFE

All young fans can feel part of Aston Villa by becoming members of JV-Life – a fantastic junior membership for youngsters 14 and under.

JV-Life, the coolest club in town, is fronted by Villa's mascots, Hercules, Bella and Chip, and there are two levels of membership – a **free online e-membership** and a full membership, which offers you some **amazing gifts**.

Full JV-Life members receive some great offers in the post, and there are also some brilliant benefits.

Members receive these items in a welcome pack:

- A welcome letter from Hercules
- An official JV-Life certificate
- A membership card
- Superhero's wristband – as worn by Hercules, Bella and Chip
- A copy of the JV-Life comic, which is published four times a season
- An exclusive watch
- Amazing match ticket offers

Colour in Hercules' spinning ball!

Members also receive a **birthday card** and **Christmas card** from our three superheroes.

And your membership card entitles you to **10% off merchandise** in the club shop plus **10% off stadium tours** and certain Villa events.

There are also dedicated events for members, including the **JV-Life Christmas party.** Last year it was held at Birmingham's Sealife Centre and everyone had a brilliant time.

Apart from the incredible experience of the Sealife Centre, members also had **visits from Bella, Hercules and Chip as well as Santa Claus and Villa players** Marc Albrighton and Eric Lichaj.

All this costs just £19.95 for a whole year – and junior season ticket holders receive complimentary membership!

ONLY £19.95 per year!

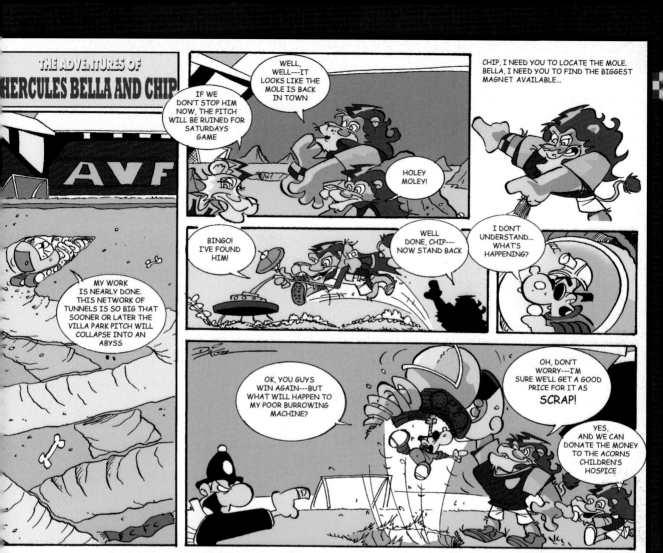

47

SHIRT STORY...

Villa's players have worn claret and blue kit for most of the club's existence, although there have been numerous variations on the design.

While a predominantly claret shirt with blue sleeves is undoubtedly what we have come to accept as the traditional Villa kit, the design has been tweaked over the years – and on occasions we have had plain claret shirts or even stripes.

Here's a selection of Villa kits over the past three decades, courtesy of John Devlin, who has published two books – *True Colours* volumes one and two – which are devoted to the subject of football clubs' kits. John's website - www.truecoloursfootballkits.com.

1983-84

1986-87

1987-88

1992-93

1993-94

1997-98

1999-2000

2001-02

2003-04

2004-05

2009-10

2006-07

49

DESIGN A VILLA KIT

If you feel inspired by the kits on the previous two pages, why not have a go at designing your very own Villa kit?

Here's the outline for you – all you need are your crayons or coloured pencils to make it come alive!

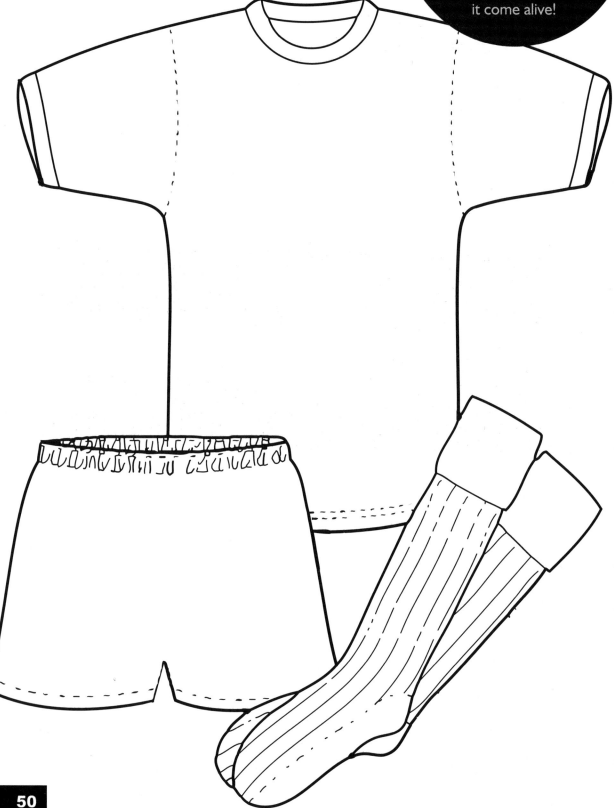

BE A VILLA EXPERT

Impress your friends with your knowledge of Villa's history. Here are a few vital Villa facts...

LIGHTING-UP TIME

Villa Park's first floodlights were installed in the summer of 1958, and used for the first time against Portsmouth on Monday 25th August.

The lights, housed on four tall pylons at each corner of the ground, were switched on at half-time in a game which Villa won 3-2.

ON THE SPOT

Villa were awarded 17 penalties in open play during the 2009-10 season – more than ever before. They converted 12 of them, with five either missed or saved.

GABBY'S HIGH5

Gabby Agbonlahor scored in five consecutive games in the early stages of the 2009-10 season – the first time a Villa player had achieved the feat since David Platt in 1990.

CHARLIE CAPS THE LOT

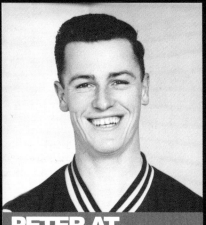

PETER AT THE DOUBLE

THE GREAT DANE!

Villa's oldest-ever scorer was a goalkeeper!

Danish keeper Peter Schmeichel was a month short of his 38th birthday when he scored a late goal in a 3-2 defeat at Everton in 2001.

The club's youngest scorer was Walter Hazelden, who netted at the age of 16 against Albion in November 1957.

Charlie Aitken has made more appearances for Villa than any other player. The Scottish footballer played a total of 660 league and cup games between 1961 and 1976. The club's record scorer is Billy Walker, who netted 244 league and cup goals between 1920 and 1933, when he retired from football.

Peter McParland was Villa's two-goal hero when we last won the FA Cup in 1957. The Irishman was on target twice in the second half at Wembley to give Villa a 2-1 victory over Manchester United. It was the club's seventh FA Cup triumph, and we have also won the league title seven times.

WIN WITH VILLA

Grab a die and counters for you and your friends and see who will become Villa champions! (Watch out for relegation though!)

CHAMPIONS!

		28	27	1959 - RELEGATE **GO BACK** 26
LEAGUE CUP WINNERS **MOVE ON 2** 21	22	1983 - EUROPEAN SUPER CUP **MOVE ON 4** 23	24	1987 - RELEGAT **GO TO NUMBER** 25
20	1970 - DOWN TO DIVISION THREE **BACK TO START** 19	18	17	16
11	2001 - INTERTOTO CUP **MOVE ON 1** 12	13	1960 - 2ND DIVISION CHAMPIONS **MOVE ON 4** 14	1981 - CHAMPIO **MOVE ON** 15
10	1982 - EUROPEAN CUP WINNERS **MOVE ON 4** 09	1936 - RELEGATED **GO BACK 2** 08	07	06
START! 01	02	03	1897 - DOUBLE WINNERS **MOVE ON 3** 04	05

stiliyan
PETROV

"NUTS ABOUT VILLA" COOKIES

These are simply delicious and you do not need to bake them -it's all done in five minutes in a saucepan! Please ask an adult to help you.

INGREDIENTS

2 cups of sugar
Half cup of butter
Half cup of cocoa powder
Half cup of milk

Half cup of
   crunchy peanut butter
3 cups of oats
Vanilla essence

METHOD

Put the sugar, cocoa powder, milk, butter and peanut butter together in a saucepan over a medium heat. Keep stirring and allow it to boil gently for 3 minutes.

Turn off the heat and add the oats & a few drops of vanilla essence. Stir well. Leave to cool for 10 minutes.

While you are waiting, take a large baking tray and grease lightly. When the mixture is cool, take a teaspoon and put each small pile of the mixture on the baking tray, leaving space in between them, because they spread out a bit.

Allow to cool completely, and serve to your friends without eating them all yourself (even though that will be hard)!

ALLERGY ADVICE: This recipe contains nuts.

james
COLLINS

IT'S A [FACT]

GABBY'S GOALS

Dwight Yorke is Villa's highest Premier League scorer with 60 goals.

Gabby Agbonlahor moved into second place ahead of Dion Dublin when he scored a stoppage-time winner at West Ham in April.

It was Gabby's 49th league goal for Villa.

BRAD THE DAD

Brad Friedel is now officially Villa's oldest-ever player.

The American keeper was 39 years and 259 days when he played against Manchester United in February 2011, beating the record previously held by Ernie "Mush" Callaghan for more than half a century. Friedel subsequently became Villa's first 40-year-old player when he faced Liverpool in the final game of the season, four days after his birthday.

WALKERS WONDERS

Only two players have scored when making their Villa debut in an FA Cup-tie – and both are called Walker.

Billy Walker, the club's record scorer, netted twice against QPR in his first game for the club in 1920 – and right-back Kyle Walker was on target when he scored Villa's first goal in a 3-1 victory over Sheffield United at Bramall Lane in January.

STAN'S THE MAN

Skipper Stiliyan Petrov, known to his team-mates as "Stan", became only the second player to win his 100th international cap while playing for Villa.

Stiliyan reached his century in a European Championship qualifier against Switzerland in March. Ironically, the only other player to achieve the feat was also nicknamed Stan! Steve Staunton won his 100th cap for the Republic of Ireland during the 2002 World Cup finals.

4 .in one

Did you hear the one about the Irishman, the Frenchman and the two Scots?

No, this isn't a joke – Villa had four different managers throughout the course of 2010-11. Martin O'Neill was in charge for all the pre-season games, and after the Irishman resigned, Scot Kevin MacDonald became caretaker boss for the opening seven league and cup games. Gerard Houllier was then appointed to the post and when the Frenchman was taken ill in April, a second Scot – assistant manager Gary McAllister – took over for the remaining five games.

100 seasons, 742 players

Last season was Villa's 100th in top flight football and by the end of the campaign a total of 742 players had represented the club in either 1st Division or Premier League games.

The 12 new boys in 2010-11 were Barry Bannan, Nathan Baker, Darren Bent, Michael Bradley, Chris Herd, Jonathan Hogg, Stephen Ireland, Eric Lichaj, Jean II Makoun, Robert Pires, Kyle Walker and Andreas Weimann.

BLACK COUNTRY BLUES

All good things come to an end, as we discovered last season. It had been 31 years since the boys in claret and blue last lost to Wolves and 26 since they had been beaten by West Bromwich Albion.

But Wolves won 1-0 at Villa Park in March and the Baggies came out on top 2-1 at The Hawthorns a few weeks later.

At least Villa had beaten both of their Black Country rivals earlier in the season!

CRUCIAL TRIO FOR JAMES

James Collins maintained his record of scoring crucial goals for Villa during the 2010-11 campaign. The former West Ham central defender was on target only three times but each goal was vital.

One was a stoppage-time header in a 3-2 home win over Blackpool, another a late equaliser for a 1-1 draw against Birmingham City in the Second City derby at St Andrew's and the third a header which clinched a 1-0 victory over Newcastle United.

LIONS FOR CLUB & COUNTRY

Did you know that Villa have provided more England internationals than any other club?

The figure at the end of last season stood at an impressive 71, and hopefully we will see even more players proudly wearing Villa's lion and the three lions on England's shirt during the next few years.

Darren Bent, the club's record signing from Sunderland, had the distinction of becoming the 70th Villa player to represent England when he lined up in a friendly against Denmark in Copenhagen last month. And on the same night Stewart Downing became Villa's 71st England international when he went on as a substitute for Arsenal's Theo Walcott.

It was very much a claret and blue night at the Parken Stadium, because Bent scored England's first goal in a 2-1 win – and another Villa player, Ashley Young, hit the winner after replacing Wayne Rooney at half-time.

The Villa connection didn't end with the three Lions who represented the Three Lions on the night. Full-back Kyle Walker was also in the squad who travelled to Denmark, while Gabby Agbonlahor was originally selected by manager Fabio Capello but withdrew for family reasons.

Villa have been providing players for the national team since 1882, when Howard Vaughton and Arthur Brown were selected for a match against Ireland in Belfast. Not only that, Vaughton scored five times and Brown four in a runaway 13-0 England win!

Villa's most-capped England international is Gareth Southgate who made 42 appearances for the national side during his time with the club.

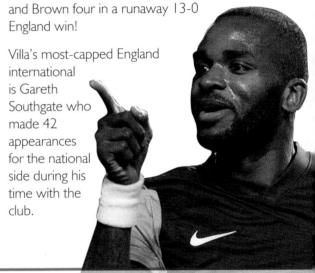

THE ENGLAND CONNECTION

Player	Year	Player	Year	Player	Year
ARTHUR BROWN	1882	ANDY DUCAT	1920	PETER WITHE	1981-84
H. VAUGHTON	1882-84	BILLY WALKER	1920-32	NIGEL SPINK	1983
OLIVER WHATELEY	1883	BILLY KIRTON	1921	GORDON COWANS	1983-90
ALBERT ALLEN	1888	FRANK MOSS	1921-24	STEVE HODGE	1986
D. HODGETTS	1888-94	TOMMY SMART	1921-29	DAVID PLATT	1989
C. ATHERSMITH	1892-00	DICKIE YORK	1922-26	TONY DALEY	1991-92
JOHN DEVEY	1892-94	G. BLACKBURN	1924	EARL BARRETT	1993
JOHN REYNOLDS	1894-97	ARTHUR DORRELL	1924-25	K. RICHARDSON	1994
STEVE SMITH	1895	TOMMY MORT	1924-26	G. SOUTHGATE	1995-02
JIMMY CRABTREE	1896-02	BEN OLNEY	1928	UGO EHIOGU	1996
H. SPENCER	1897-05	ERIC HOUGHTON	1930-31	STAN COLLYMORE	1997
FRED WHELDON	1897-98	JOE TATE	1931-32	DION DUBLIN	1998
ALBERT WILKES	1901-02	T. 'PONGO' WARING	1931-32	LEE HENDRIE	1998
BILLY GEORGE	1902	GEORGE BROWN	1932	PAUL MERSON	1998
BILLY GARRATY	1903	RONNIE STARLING	1933-37	GARETH BARRY	2000-09
JOE BACHE	1903-11	JOE BERESFORD	1934	DAVID JAMES	2001
BILLY BRAWN	1904	TOMMY GARDNER	1934-35	DARIUS VASSELL	2002-04
ALEX LEAKE	1904-05	FRANK BROOME	1938-39	ASHLEY YOUNG	2007-11
ALBERT HALL	1910	EDDIE LOWE	1947	G. AGBONLAHOR	2008-10
HARRY HAMPTON	1913-14	T. THOMPSON	1951	EMILE HESKEY	2009-10
CHARLIE WALLACE	1913-20	GERRY HITCHENS	1961	JAMES MILNER	2008-10
SAM HARDY	1914-20	BRIAN LITTLE	1975	S. WARNOCK	2009
FRANK BARSON	1920	JOHN GIDMAN	1977	S. DOWNING	2011
		TONY MORLEY	1981-82	DARREN BENT	2011

FIND THE STRIKERS

Villa have had some great strikers down the years, including current Holte End hero Darren Bent. But just imagine if we could have a whole team of strikers!

You will find Bent plus 11 other Villa hot-shots in this wordsearch. The names can go across the grid, backwards, downwards and diagonally.

These are the names you are looking for:

BENT	SAUNDERS	SHAW
GRAY	YORKE	HITCHENS
McPARLAND	DUBLIN	ANGEL
WITHE	LITTLE	HATELEY

```
M L X A Z E W A H S
O C E L T T I L F A
H Y P B C N T D R U
I G R A Y X H S E N
T V Y O R K E W F D
C B E N T L F J T E
H G L E G N A M U R
E D R S A U C N E S
N V K N I L B U D O
S Q H A T E L E Y L
```

To check if you're right, have a look on page 61.

ANSWERS

PUZZLED? - PAGE 32

ODD ONE OUT

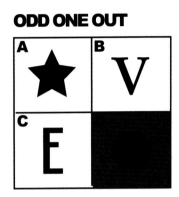

SUDOKU

4	2	3	1
1	3	2	4
3	1	4	2
2	4	1	3

MAZE

THE DEBUT DOZEN - PAGE 34

1. BARRY BANNAN
2. STEPHEN IRELAND
3. CHRIS HERD
4. DARREN BENT
5. ANDREAS WEIMANN
6. ROBERT PIRES
7. JEAN MAKOUN
8. ERIC LICHAJ
9. NATHAN BAKER
10. MICHAEL BRADLEY
11. KYLE WALKER
12. JONATHAN HOGG